STARS&
PLANETS

Dr Mike Goldsmith

KINGFISHER

First published 2008 by Kingfisher
This edition published 2015 by Kingfisher
an imprint of Macmillan Children's Books
20 New Wharf Road, London N1 9RR
Associated companies throughout the world
www.panmacmillan.com

Illustration by Chris Moore (represented by Artist Partners Ltd), Alex Pang and The Peter Bull Art Studio

ISBN 978-0-7534-3981-4

9 8 7 6 5 4 3 2 1

1TR/0815/WKT/UNTD/128MA

A CIP catalogue record for this book is available from the British Library.

Printed in China

Note to readers: The website addresses listed in this book are correct at the time of publishing.
However, due to the ever-changing nature of the internet, website addresses and content can change.
Websites can contain links that are unsuitable for children. The publisher cannot be held responsible for
changes in website addresses or content, or for information obtained through third-party websites.
We strongly advise that internet searches should be supervised by an adult.

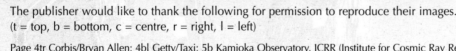

The publisher would like to thank the following for permission to reproduce their images.
(t = top, b = bottom, c = centre, r = right, l = left)

Page 4tr Corbis/Bryan Allen; 4bl Getty/Taxi; 5b Kamioka Observatory, ICRR (Institute for Cosmic Ray Research), The University of Tokyo, Japan; 8br Science Photo Library (SPL)/Jerry Lodriguss; 9bl SPL/David A. Hardy, Futures: 50 Yrs in Space; 9br SPL/Allan Morton/Dennis Milon; 10l SPL/International Astronomical Union/Martin Kornmesser; 10cl SPL/US Geological Survey; 10c SPL/NASA; 11tr SPL/Claus Lunau/FOCI/Bonnier Publications; 11bl SPL/Detlev van Ravenswaay; 11c SPL/Mark Garlick; 11br SPL/Friedrich Saurer; 12b Arcticphoto/Ragnar Sigurdsson; 12–13 SPL/Mehau Kulkyk; 13tl Tim Van Sant, ST9 Solar Sail Team Lead, NASA Goddard Space Flight Center; 13c SPL/Scharmer et al, Royal Swedish Academy of Sciences; 13cb Corbis/Roger Ressmeyer; 13r SPL; 14t ESA/NASA; 14c SPL/US Geological Survey; 15tr SPL/NASA; 16tr SPL/Bernard Edmaier; 16c SPL/Colin Cuthbert; 17tl Corbis/Keren Su; 17c PA/AP; 17c and 17cr Corbis/Randy Wells; 17bl Alamy/Steve Bloom Images; 19tr SPL/NASA; 20tl Corbis/NASA/epa; 20cl Corbis/Reuters/NASA; 20cr SPL/NASA; 21tr Corbis/ Guido Cozzi; 22cl SPL/Mark Garlick; 23b SPL/Detlev van Ravenswaay; 24t Corbis/Dennis di Cicco; 24br SPL/Detlev van Ravenswaay; 25tr Corbis/Jonathan Blair; 26bl SPL/J-C Cuillandre/Canada-France-Hawaii Telescope; 28tr SPL/Mark Garlick; 29tr SPL/Mark Garlick; 30cr SPL/NASA/ESA/R. Sahai & J. Trauger, JPL; 31tr SPL/Russell Kightley; 31b SPL/Konstantinos Kifondis; 34cl Corbis/Sergei Chirikov/epa; 34r SPL/NASA; 35tr Novosti; 35cl Corbis/NASA; 36 SPL/NASA; 37tl SPL/NASA; 37bl Corbis/Jim Sugar; 37br SPL/Lockheed Martin Corp./NASA; 38c SPL/Victor Habbick Visions; 40tr SPL/Julian Baum; 43b SPL/NASA; 48tr Getty Images/Science Faction; 48cl Science Museum Library; 48cr Alamy/Karl Johaentges; 48b SPL/NASA.

CONTENTS

4 STAR-GAZING

6 THE UNIVERSE

8 GALAXIES

10 THE SOLAR SYSTEM

12 THE SUN

14 MERCURY AND VENUS

16 EARTH

18 MARS

20 JUPITER AND SATURN

22 URANUS AND NEPTUNE

24 SPACE RUBBLE

26 SPACE CLOUDS

28 STRANGE STARS

30 STAR DEATH

32 SPACE WARPS

34 SPACE PIONEERS

36 BEYOND THE SKY

38 CITIES IN THE SKY

40 STARSHIPS

42 LIFE BEYOND

44 GLOSSARY

46 INDEX

48 INVESTIGATE

STAR-GAZING

For thousands of years, people have gazed at the starlit sky and asked questions. And for centuries, telescopes have shown them the answers – and raised more questions. When trying to understand strange planets and distant stars, scientists use images sent by telescopes, both those on Earth and those that drift through space high above us.

Observatory

In the desert of Arizona, USA, Kitt Peak National Observatory is home to 19 optical telescopes. The telescopes use huge mirrors to gather light from stars and form images of them.

Solar panels convert sunlight into electricity to power the Hubble.

Radio telescope

There are many types of light that we cannot see but special telescopes can. This one, in Hawaii, picks up radio waves from the stars. The photograph took many minutes to make. During that time, the stars appeared to circle in the sky as Earth spun on its axis.

Hubble Space Telescope

Many of our best photographs of space are produced by this optical telescope. The Hubble has been in orbit since 1990, when it travelled into space onboard a space shuttle. It produces much clearer images than Earth-based telescopes can. The motion of air in Earth's atmosphere blurs images (causing stars to appear to twinkle). Floating beyond our atmosphere, the Hubble does not have this problem.

The 'forward shell' houses the primary mirror, which collects light and reflects it towards a secondary mirror. This mirror focuses the light onto detectors to create an image.

 The light from most stars takes years to reach us. A star looks as it was long before you were born.

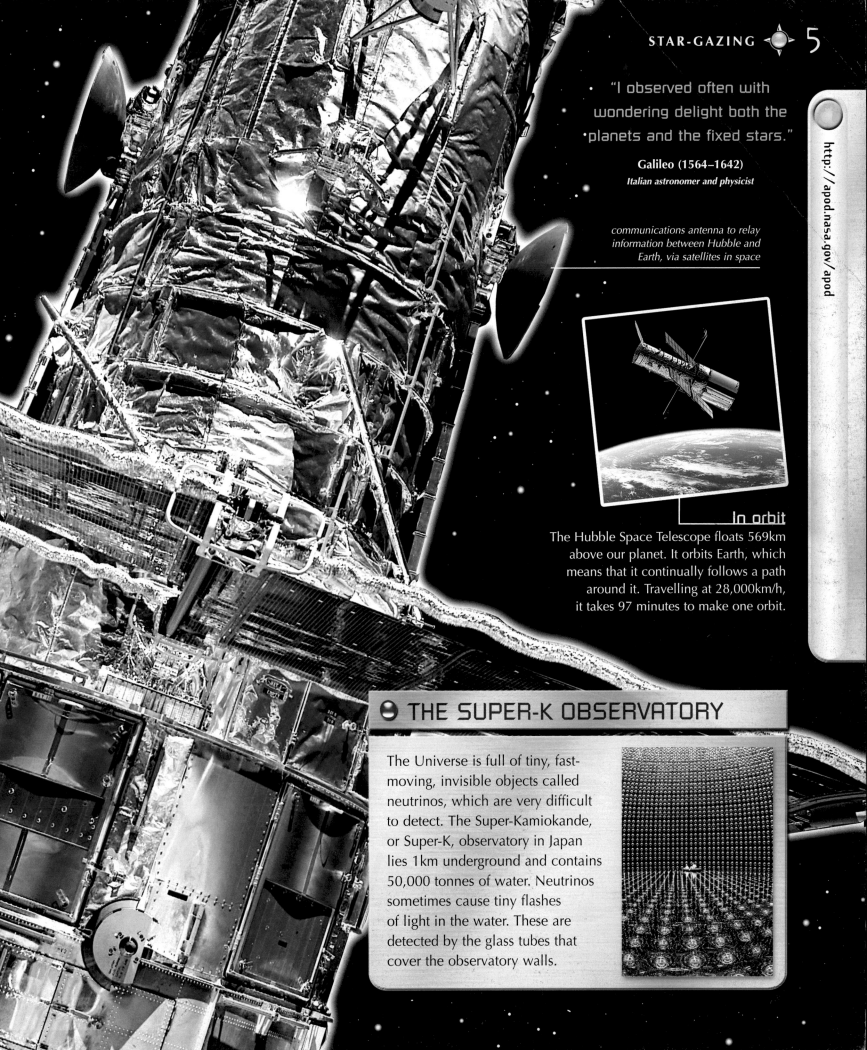

"I observed often with wondering delight both the planets and the fixed stars."

Galileo (1564–1642)
Italian astronomer and physicist

communications antenna to relay information between Hubble and Earth, via satellites in space

http://apod.nasa.gov/apod

In orbit

The Hubble Space Telescope floats 569km above our planet. It orbits Earth, which means that it continually follows a path around it. Travelling at 28,000km/h, it takes 97 minutes to make one orbit.

☻ THE SUPER-K OBSERVATORY

The Universe is full of tiny, fast-moving, invisible objects called neutrinos, which are very difficult to detect. The Super-Kamiokande, or Super-K, observatory in Japan lies 1km underground and contains 50,000 tonnes of water. Neutrinos sometimes cause tiny flashes of light in the water. These are detected by the glass tubes that cover the observatory walls.

THE UNIVERSE

About 13.7 billion years ago, the Universe began – time, space and energy appeared, and space expanded rapidly. That expansion, and the fading flash of the beginning of everything, still continue today.

When the Universe was cool enough, tiny particles of matter and antimatter formed. By the end of the first second, most of these particles had destroyed each other.

The matter that remained was not spread evenly through space. Gradually, the gravity of the denser areas attracted more matter, further increasing their density. Galaxies would later form in these areas, which are shown below in blue.

electrons and anti-electrons created in a laboratory (this happened naturally in the early Universe)

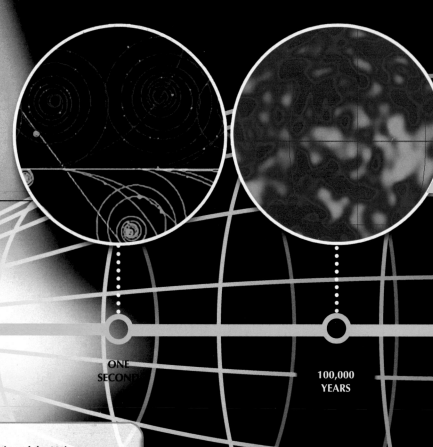

The cause of the Big Bang is science's greatest unsolved mystery.

The Universe underwent a sudden jump in the rate of its expansion.

ZERO TIME

LESS THAN ONE TRILLIONTH OF A SECOND

ONE SECOND

100,000 YEARS

Dark matter and dark energy

Most of the Universe is invisible because every galaxy is loaded with dark matter, which may consist of particles of an unknown type. The whole of space is filled with dark energy, a mysterious force that opposes the pull of gravity.

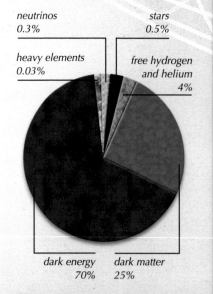

The composition of the Universe

neutrinos 0.3%

stars 0.5%

heavy elements 0.03%

free hydrogen and helium 4%

dark energy 70%

dark matter 25%

The blue glow is dark matter; the pink area is ordinary matter.

"The size and age of the cosmos are beyond ordinary human understanding. Lost somewhere between immensity and eternity is our tiny planetary home."

Carl Sagan (1934–1996)
American astronomer and astrochemist

> The Sun is about one third of the age of the Universe.

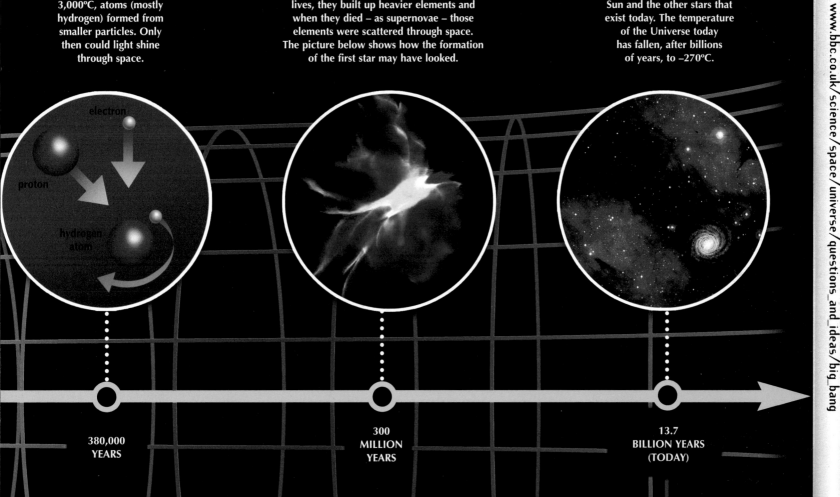

When the Universe had cooled to about 3,000ºC, atoms (mostly hydrogen) formed from smaller particles. Only then could light shine through space.

The first generation of stars formed from hydrogen and helium. During their lives, they built up heavier elements and when they died – as supernovae – those elements were scattered through space. The picture below shows how the formation of the first star may have looked.

The heavy elements from the first stars form part of the Sun and the other stars that exist today. The temperature of the Universe today has fallen, after billions of years, to –270ºC.

electron

proton

hydrogen atom

380,000 YEARS

300 MILLION YEARS

13.7 BILLION YEARS (TODAY)

The early Universe changed very rapidly, and then the pace of change slowed, so this timeline of key events is not to scale.

⊖ THE BIG CHILL AND THE BIG RIP

There are two main theories about the future of the Universe. It may continue to expand indefinitely, slowing but never stopping. All the stars would burn out until everything became dark and cold – a Big Chill. However, there are signs and theories that the rate of the Universe's expansion is increasing. One day, galaxies, stars, planets and atoms may all tear themselves apart – a Big Rip.

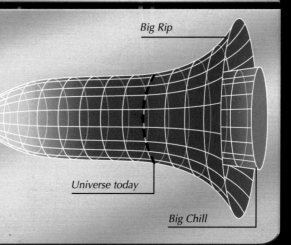

Big Rip

Big Bang

Universe today

Big Chill

GALAXIES

Stars are not spread evenly throughout the Universe – they are grouped into galaxies, each one containing millions, billions or trillions of stars. Many galaxies are like gigantic whirlpools of stars, while others are more like discs, or balls, or softly glowing clouds of light.

New stars are born in the spiral arms of this galaxy.

A dwarf galaxy

No one knows for sure how galaxies form, but it may be that they begin life like this young galaxy, which is much smaller than our own. The red glow in the centre is the light of ancient stars, while young new ones burn blue in the outer regions.

The Whirlpool Galaxy

In spiral galaxies like this, the curving arms, which are marked by lanes of thick black dust, are regions of starbirth. Like most other galaxies, the Whirlpool Galaxy is rushing away from us as the Universe expands and the distances between galaxies grow. Every second, the galaxy is 500km further away.

Andromeda spiral

This galaxy is the most distant thing we can see with the naked eye. It is a trillion times brighter than the Sun, but so far away (2.5 million light-years) that it can be seen only on the darkest of nights.

 Billions of years ago, most galaxies were blue due to the large number of stars forming in them.

www.damtp.cam.ac.uk/research/gr/public/gal_home.html

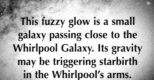

This fuzzy glow is a small galaxy passing close to the Whirlpool Galaxy. Its gravity may be triggering starbirth in the Whirlpool's arms.

Galaxies shine with both visible and invisible radiation. This photograph shows not just visible light but also ultraviolet radiation from new stars in the outer ring and heat radiation from older stars in the core.

⊖ OUR GALAXY – THE MILKY WAY

Our Sun and the Solar System lie in one of the Milky Way's outer arms.

From the side, the galaxy would look flat, with the yellow nucleus of older stars bulging at its centre.

The milky stripe of light in our night sky is our own galaxy, the Milky Way, seen from the inside. The galaxy contains billions of stars, and orbiting some of them are planets that may be similar to those in our own solar system.

The Milky Way appears brighter from the Southern Hemisphere, as the South Pole points roughly towards the bright galactic core.

THE SOLAR SYSTEM

The Sun's web of gravity stretches far out into space, and caught in that web are the planets, moons, rubble and dust that make up the Solar System. Everything in it moves continually around the Sun, with gravity and velocity (motion) in perfect balance.

GRAVITY – the force that pulls all objects towards one another

Building blocks

The inner planets are composed mainly of rock and metal, while the outer planets are mostly ice and gas. This is because when the Sun began to shine, the inner regions of the Solar System became so hot that only rock and metal worlds could survive there.

MERCURY
(first reached by
Mariner 10 *in 1974)*

Volume: 0.06 Earths
Mass: 0.06 Earths
Day length: 176 Earth-days
Year length: 88 Earth-days

EARTH
Volume: 1.09×10^{12}km^3
Mass: 5.98×10^{24}kg
Day length: 24h
Year length: 365.24 days

MARS
(first reached by
Mariner 4 *in 1965)*

Volume: 0.15 Earths
Mass: 0.11 Earths
Day length: 24h 37min
Year length: 687 Earth-days

JUPITER
(first reached by
Pioneer 10 *in 1973)*

Volume: 1,266 Earths
Mass: 318 Earths
Day length: 9h 55min
Year length: 12 Earth-years

VENUS
(first reached by
Mariner 2 *in 1962)*

Volume: 0.85 Earths
Mass: 0.82 Earths
Day length: 117 Earth-days
Year length: 225 Earth-days

Distances from the Sun

The planets closer to the Sun are also closer to each other. The Solar System began life as a cloud of dust and gas, and the Sun formed in its densest area. So the region nearest to our star had more materials with which to build planets.

Earth
150
million km

Venus
108
million km

Mars
228
million km

Jupiter
778
million km

SUN

Saturn
1,427
million km

Mercury
58
million km

If we were able to step outside the Solar System and look at it as a whole, the sunlit realm of the planets would be too tiny to see. Beyond the planets lies the ring-shaped Kuiper Belt, which is made up of icy objects. The Kuiper Belt merges into the Oort Cloud, an enormous area shaped like a hollow sphere, which contains the cores of comets. The whole Solar System is about two light-years across.

empty region

cross-section of
the Oort Cloud, which
surrounds the Solar System

"We have swept through
all of the planets in the Solar
System, from Mercury to Neptune,
in a historic 20 [to] 30 year age
of spacecraft discovery."

Carl Sagan (1934–1996)
American astronomer and astrochemist

www.valdosta.edu/~cbarnbau/astro_demos/stellar_evol/birth.html

SATURN
(first reached by
Pioneer 11 *in 1979)*

Volume: 752 Earths
Mass: 95 Earths
Day length: 10h 39min
Year length: 29.5 Earth-years

NEPTUNE
(first reached by
Voyager 2 *in 1989)*

Volume: 59 Earths
Mass: 17 Earths
Day length: 16h 7min
Year length: 165 Earth-years

URANUS
(first reached by
Voyager 2 *in 1986)*

Volume: 64 Earths
Mass: 15 Earths
Day length: 17h 14min
Year length: 84 Earth-years

Uranus
2,871
million km

Neptune
4,497
million km

THE SUN

Our Sun is a vast ball of glowing gas, so large that a million Earths would fit inside it. Without its light and heat, there would be no life on Earth, and even our atmosphere would lie frozen solid on the ground. Although it is 150 million kilometres away, its light is still bright enough to damage our eyes. As the world spins around each day, the Sun moves across our skies.

SUN – our star, around which Earth and the other planets of our solar system orbit

Nuclear furnace

The Sun is made mostly of a light substance called hydrogen. Deep in its core, reactions like those in nuclear bombs convert the hydrogen into helium and release the enormous energy that we see as sunlight.

Light shows

The Sun sends out tiny particles, as well as light and heat. Near the north and south poles of Earth, these particles are caught in our planet's magnetic field, producing strange, coloured lights in the night sky. These spectacular displays are called aurorae.

Every second, the Sun becomes 4 million tonnes lighter.

Sun sailing

The Sun's light gently presses against everything it touches. Solar sails are light and shiny craft that drift through space, pushed by sunlight as sailing ships are pushed by wind.

Solar prominence

A prominence is a gigantic cloud of glowing gas – much larger than Earth – that floats in the Sun's atmosphere.

Sunspots are dark patches caused by the Sun's powerful magnetic field. They are darker than the rest of the Sun because they are cooler.

"One result of the evolution of our Sun... will very likely be the reduction of our Earth to a bleak, charred cinder."

Carl Sagan (1934–1996)
American astronomer and astrochemist

The temperature of the Sun's surface is about 5,500ºC.

Solar eclipse

Every few months, the Moon passes directly between the Sun and Earth. When this happens, the Sun seems to turn black, and the glow of its corona appears around it (see right). At other times, the corona is too dim to see against the Sun's bright light.

www.nasa.gov/vision/universe/solarsystem/sun_for_kids_main.html

MERCURY AND VENUS

Mercury and Venus are much closer to the Sun than we are, which means they are much hotter than Earth. They also move more quickly round the Sun than we do, so their years are shorter than ours.

Colourful craters?

Like many photographs taken in space, this *Mariner 10* image has been falsely coloured to show the different features more clearly.

metal-rich area

solidified lava flow

Kuiper crater

No data has been recorded for this area, so it is left blank in images of the planet.

Mercury

Mercury, the smallest planet and the closest to the Sun, cools rapidly at night because it has almost no atmosphere. So, while the temperature can reach 430°C by day, nights are colder than Antarctica. This image pieces together photographs taken by the *Mariner 10* probe, which travelled to Mercury in 1974. It discovered that the planet is rocky and heavily cratered.

The surface of Mercury is marked with wrinkles. These probably formed when the planet cooled and shrunk soon after it formed.

> Although Mercury is much closer to the Sun than Venus, it is Venus that is the hotter planet.

Mapping Venus

The thick clouds of Venus always hide its surface from our telescopes. So, in 1989, the Magellan probe was sent to orbit the planet and map it by radar. It revealed that all of Venus's surface is young – only half a billion years old.

Lava domes

Many of the features that Magellan discovered on Venus are caused by volcanic activity. These domes are like nothing known on any other planet. They may have been caused by lava welling up under the ground, causing the surface to stretch and rise.

The Magellan probe orbited Venus for four years.

Only flashes of lightning brighten Venus's cloudy, dark surface.

The 3-D maps of Venus produced by the Magellan probe show that most of its rocky surface is made up of smooth volcanic plains.

Maat Mons, the highest volcano on Venus

Venus

Venus, our nearest neighbour, was once thought to be similar to Earth in prehistoric times. In fact, Venus is a deadly planet with an atmosphere as dense as a liquid. Rains of sulphuric acid fall from the cloudy, yellow sky, boiling away before reaching the ground. The greenhouse effect heats the planet's surface to 480°C.

www.space.com/mercury and http://nssdc.gsfc.nasa.gov/photo_gallery/

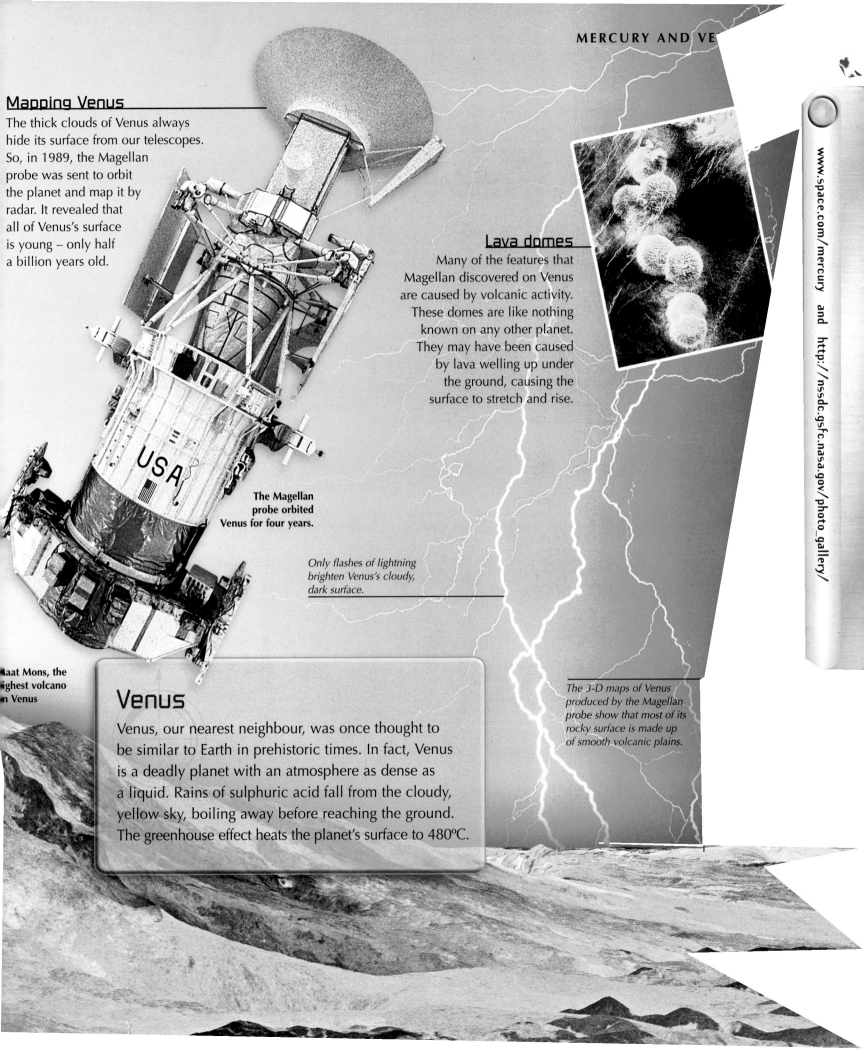

EARTH

The distance of Earth from the Sun is what makes life on our planet possible. Living things need liquid water, and if we were much further from the Sun, all our water would be frozen as it is on Mars. If we were a little closer, water would boil as it would on Venus.

As the world is gradually heating up, our polar ice is melting. This causes flooding in low-lying areas.

Plants and trees produce oxygen, which all animals need to breathe. Plants also absorb the waste gases that animals breathe out.

Earth's atmosphere

An atmosphere is the layer of gases held around a planet by the force of its gravity. Earth's atmospheric gases keep the surface warm at night and protect it from dangerous Sun rays during the day. The atmosphere also helps to move water around. When water evaporates from the oceans, clouds form in the lowest layer of the atmosphere. The clouds bring rain to the land.

"We do not inherit the Earth from our ancestors, we borrow it from our children."

Haida Indian saying

LIQUID – a state of matter in which a substance is runny, taking the shape of its container and forming a surface inside it

> If all the ice on Earth melted, the seas would rise by 100m.

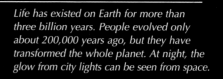

Life has existed on Earth for more than three billion years. People evolved only about 200,000 years ago, but they have transformed the whole planet. At night, the glow from city lights can be seen from space.

⊖ THE SEASONS

Because Earth tilts on its axis, while one hemisphere is angled towards the Sun, the other hemisphere is angled away from it. So, when one hemisphere experiences summer, the other has winter. These seasons change as Earth completes its yearly orbit of the Sun. Night and day are caused by Earth spinning on its axis – it takes 24 hours for the planet to complete one rotation.

The Northern Hemisphere, angled away from the Sun, experiences winter.

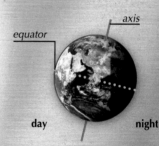

axis

equator

day   night

The Southern Hemisphere, angled towards the Sun, experiences summer.

Shifting plates

Deep beneath your feet, Earth is so hot that the rock is liquid. On this fiery sea, vast areas of stone, called plates, float. As the plates slowly crunch into each other, they cause volcanoes and earthquakes.

There are over two million species of life on Earth, each adapted to live in a particular place, like these penguins in their frozen home.

MARS

Mars, the 'red planet', has fascinated people for more than a century. It is the second-closest planet to us and is the planet most like our own, with ice caps, seasons, volcanoes and deserts. Long ago, it had lakes and rivers, too. In August 2012, NASA succeeded in landing a rover called *Curiosity* on Mars. *Curiosity* is investigating the possibility of life on Mars, and will provide much more data about the red planet than we have ever had before.

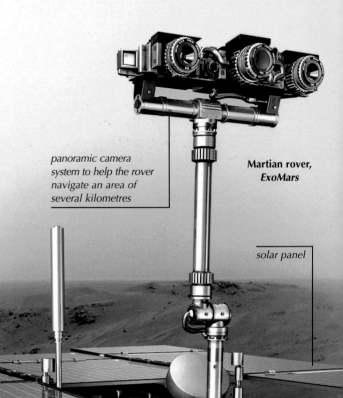

panoramic camera system to help the rover navigate an area of several kilometres

Martian rover, *ExoMars*

solar panel

six rugged wheels to cope with the planet's rocky terrain

In 1976, a probe, *Viking 2*, landed on Mars and took this photograph. It shows a pink sky, caused by the red dust particles in the air.

ExoMars

The *ExoMars* rover is due to begin its exploration of the red planet in 2016 as part of a European Space Agency (ESA) project. The rover will be delivered by an orbiter, and will use balloons or parachutes to slow its descent and land safely. The rover will continue studies of the planet's rocks, building on *Viking 2*'s discovery that Martian soil is full of chemicals that would burn human skin.

 > Mars is red because it is rusty. Long ago, iron in its desert soil combined with oxygen and painted the whole world red.

⊖ ICE ON MARS

This bright-blue patch is a frozen pool of ice. It lies in a crater on Mars's vast northern plains. The photograph was taken by ESA's *Mars Express Orbiter* in 2005. Water cannot exist in liquid form because the planet's atmospheric pressure is currently too low.

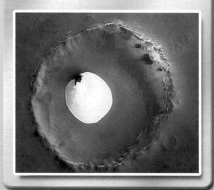

antenna to communicate with Earth

This instrument uses radar waves to 'see' up to 1km beneath the planet's surface.

solar panel to power orbiter

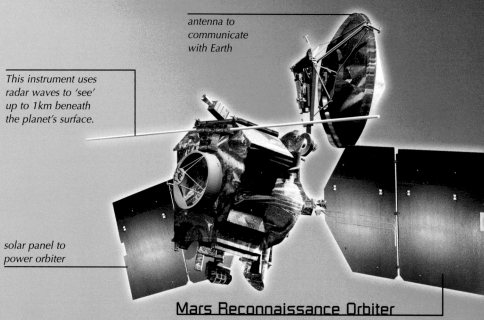

Mars Reconnaissance Orbiter

This spacecraft reached Mars in 2006 and it still circles the planet today. Its mission is to take pictures of the planet's surface, monitor the weather and study the rocks and ice. It is also looking for the best places for future spacecraft to land. One day, it will be used to pass messages from other missions back to Earth.

The frozen north

The *Reconnaissance Orbiter* took this photograph of Mars's northern polar region. It shows steep cliffs, almost 2km high, cloaked in ice.

Mars has permanently frozen ice at both its north and south poles. As on Earth, the ice caps grow or shrink according to the season.

"If [Mars rovers] find a rock that proves there was once life on Mars, it will be, without any doubt, the greatest scientific discovery ever made."

David McNab and James Younger
writers and science-documentary producers

http://mars.jpl.nasa.gov

Jupiter's Great Red Spot is a giant hurricane – much larger than Earth – that has raged for centuries.

Ganymede, the largest moon in the Solar System, is bigger than Mercury.

Callisto is made largely of ice.

Io is sprinkled with erupting volcanoes.

Europa has liquid seas under its icy crust.

JUPITER AND SATURN

Jupiter and Saturn are gas giants – huge worlds with deep atmospheres concealing cores of rock and ice. Both have rings – Jupiter's are faint dust belts, whereas Saturn's rings are made of rocky ice – and both have at least 60 moons each. The planets spin so fast that they have very short days and the flattened-sphere shape of a grapefruit. Both are still cooling from their formation, and this leftover heat generates storms that never end.

Many moons

Jupiter has at least 63 moons, many of them locked by gravity so that one side always faces the planet. Some, like Io, are warmed by the stretching and squeezing effects of Jupiter's gravity. Others crumble into space, their dust forming rings round the planet.

> Jupiter is large enough to contain all the other planets.

Jupiter

Jupiter is the giant planet of our solar system, more massive than all the others combined. Although it is more than four times as far from us as the Sun, it can be the brightest object in the night sky. Jupiter is surrounded by a zone of deadly radiation and an enormous magnetic field.

www.esa.int/esaKIDSen/SEMF8WVLWFE_OurUniverse_0.html

Light world

Although Saturn weighs more than 95 times the weight of Earth, it is still the lightest planet for its size in the Solar System. It is so light that it would float in water.

Saturn's rings are shown in false colour here. The pink rings contain only large rocks; green and blue include smaller fragments as well.

Saturn

Saturn's ring system is composed of billions of orbiting fragments of icy rock that range in size from dust particles to boulders. They may be the remains of a moon-sized object that strayed too close to Saturn and was torn apart by the planet's gravity.

URANUS AND NEPTUNE

The two outermost planets of our solar system, Uranus and Neptune, are gas giants like Jupiter and Saturn. Far out in space, the Sun shines dimly, so these worlds are cold and dark. As they move slowly around the Sun on huge orbits, they have long years – Uranus's year is 84 Earth-years long and Neptune's is 165.

ORBIT – *the path of one object around another in space*

Uranus

Uranus was discovered in 1781 by English astronomer William Herschel (1738–1822), and reached by space probe 197 years later. This giant planet, circled by dark rings of black boulders, gets its green colour from the methane in its atmosphere. Uranus spins on its back, probably knocked over by a collision with a wandering planet billions of years ago.

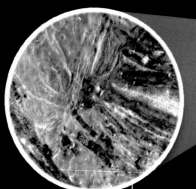

Miranda, a moon of Uranus

Miranda's surface is so jumbled that some scientists think the moon was shattered long ago and then reassembled when gravity pulled the fragments together again.

 On some parts of Uranus, night can last for more than 40 Earth-years.

Voyages to remote worlds

The twin Voyager space probes, *Voyager 1* and *Voyager 2*, explored the outer planets in the 1970s and 1980s. Both probes will travel beyond the Solar System for many thousands of years – although they will cease to function in the 2020s. In about 40,000 years, *Voyager 2* will reach a nearby star.

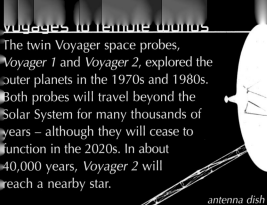

instruments to record energy and light data

generators provide electrical power

antenna dish

A magnometer on the arm measures magnetic forces.

***Voyager 2* used the gravity of Uranus to propel itself towards Neptune.**

"I saw, O, first of all mankind,
I saw the disk of my new planet gliding there
beyond our tumults, in that realm of peace."

Herschel's discovery of Uranus
from Alfred Noyes's poem The Torch-Bearers, *1937*

Vast white clouds of methane ice rush across a dark storm system on the face of Neptune, the windiest planet in the Solar System.

http://photojournal.jpl.nasa.gov/index.html

Neptune

The colour of the outermost planet in our solar system gives it its name – Neptune, god of the blue sea. Unlike the other giants, some of Neptune's rings are incomplete arcs. This cold planet generates some heat of its own and this powers its dramatic weather systems. However, its largest moon, Triton, may be the coldest moon in the Solar System.

Nitrogen, which makes up most of our air, is mainly frozen solid on Neptune's moon Triton. However, sometimes it squirts upwards as liquid jets, before being knocked sideways by high-altitude winds.

SPACE RUBBLE

As comets (lumps of grit and ice) near the Sun, their surfaces boil and crumble, releasing dusts and gases that form tails. The faint blue tail behind comet Hale-Bopp is gas; the brighter tail is dust.

The Solar System contains one star, eight planets, about 170 moons – and billions of other objects, ranging from tiny grains of dust to lumps of ice, rock or metal hundreds of kilometres wide. This rubble is the Solar System's leftover building material, and most of it has remained unchanged for thousands of millions of years. It is made up of dwarf planets, comets, meteoroids, asteroids and Kuiper Belt objects.

Shooting stars (meteors) are the trails of small pieces of falling space rubble (meteoroids) that glow as they burn up in our atmosphere.

This far above Earth, there is no atmosphere in which the asteroid can burn up. The fiery trail has been caused by nuclear missiles, sent from Earth in an attempt to destroy the asteroid.

Mimas, a moon of Saturn, was almost destroyed by the object that crashed into it and created this enormous crater.

⊖ DWARF PLANET PLUTO

Pluto and the largest of its three moons, Charon (on right)

Pluto, discovered in 1930, is one of the Solar System's three known dwarf planets, which are small round worlds. Its oval orbit means that its distance from the Sun varies greatly, and at times, Pluto is closer to the Sun than Neptune. When it is a long way out in space, Pluto becomes so cold that its atmosphere freezes solid.

> Comet Hyakutake had a tail more than 570 million km long – four times the distance between Earth and the Sun.

The destruction of Earth

Throughout its history, Earth has been the target of many asteroids. The impact of one caused the extinction of the dinosaurs, and another of a similar size could mean the end of human civilization. Scientists are tracking the orbits of asteroids – if one ever appears to be on a collision course for our planet, it might be disintegrated by nuclear weapons, or pushed or pulled off course with rockets or solar sails (see page 13).

Barringer Crater

This crater, in Arizona, USA, was formed by the impact of a meteorite about 50,000 years ago. It is about 1,200m wide.

"Our missiles have failed. The comets are still headed for Earth and there's nothing we can do to stop them...The impact is going to be... well, disastrous."

From the 1998 film *Deep Impact*

SPACE CLOUDS

When people started to study the night sky with telescopes, they found fuzzy patches, which they called nebulae, meaning clouds. Many of these nebulae really are clouds – of glowing or dark dust or gas. They are places of starbirth or star death. Other nebulae are nearby clusters of stars, and some are distant galaxies.

GAS – a state of matter in which a substance expands to fill its container

Pillars of Creation

In these vast columns of dust and gas, which form part of the Eagle Nebula, new stars are being born. Powerful radiation from hot young stars nearby heats the outer layers of the columns to form the bluish green mist that can be seen around them.

Starbirth

This telescope image shows a wider view of the Eagle Nebula with an exploding star at its glowing core. Exploding stars (supernovae) squeeze parts of surrounding cloud, creating dense regions. Gravity continues the process, and the squeezed regions get more and more dense. They also get hotter – their centres get so hot that nuclear reactions begin, turning these central areas into stars.

Small protusion contain globule of dense gas tha are the beginning of new stars

Many of the atoms we are made of spent millions of years in a molecular cloud after forming in an exploding star.

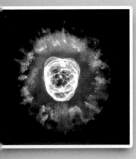

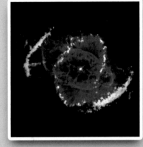

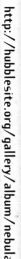http://hubblesite.org/gallery/album/nebula

At only 1,000 years old, the Eskimo Nebula is very young. Astronomer William Herschel discovered it in 1787. Later, he described spherical nebulae like the Eskimo as 'planetary nebulae'.

A planetary nebula, which is gas thrown off by a star, is usually sphere-shaped. The Cat's Eye Nebula, however, has a much more complex shape. No one is sure why.

The Crab Nebula is the remains of a supernova – a massive star exploding at the end of its life. The light from the explosion reached Earth in 1054.

The Orion Nebula is the easiest to see from Earth. This detail shows the Horsehead, a dark cloud of dust silhouetted against the glow of a hot gas cloud called an emission nebula.

ach pillar is about one ght-year long. This means at it would take light ne year to travel from e top to the bottom.

"...the nebulae [are] amazing us by the strangeness of their forms and the incomprehensibility of their nature..."

Mary Somerville (1780–1872)
Scottish science writer

The Pillars may no longer exist – a nearby supernova explosion might have destroyed them 6,000 years ago. If so, we will not see that destruction for a thousand years as the Pillars are 7,000 light-years away.

⊖ BRIGHT DUST SHELLS

Many ageing stars throw off shells of dust, and many others flash and pulse with light. These images show both: the central star has sent a burst of light that is spreading gradually through the dust shells, lighting up one after another.

The red glow at the centre of the dust shells is a supergiant star.

The black regions are holes in the dust shells.

The outermost dust shell is about the size of Jupiter.

Blue giant

A blue giant, a thousand times larger than the Sun, is as hot as a star can be without destroying itself. Its vast power boils away its atmosphere and floods the region around it with harsh blue light and deadly radiation.

STRANGE STARS

The Sun is a very ordinary star that has changed little in temperature or brightness during the history of life on Earth. This is lucky for us – if it had changed much, we would probably not be here to see it. But many other stars are strange – they pulsate, change shape, join together or blow apart. And while some are incredibly hot, others barely smoulder.

Carbon star

Some cool, red stars have atmospheres rich in carbon, which condenses around them in the form of sooty clouds. The clouds filter the light of their parent star, making its glow an even deeper red.

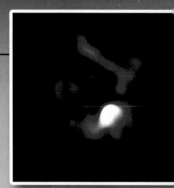

Distorted star

Not all stars are round. Mira (from the Latin for 'wonderful') looks distorted. This is either because it changes shape as it pulsates or because some of its surface is too dark to see.

 The largest known star, VY Canis Majoris, is big enough to hold about 10 billion Suns.

...inaries

...y stars – a pair of stars
...orbit each other – are very
...mon. However, it is rare to
...any that are so close that they
...ch, like these pictured here.
...rs that do touch each other,
...are each other's atmospheres
...nd distort each other's shapes.

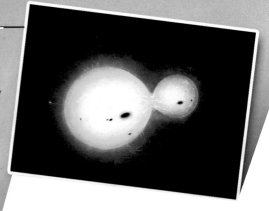

...ING DEMONS

When stars change in brightness, they are called variables. Some variable stars suddenly flash with light or are darkened by clouds of dust. Other stars brighten and dim regularly. This may be caused by other, dimmer stars orbiting them and blocking their light. The first such star to be discovered is called Algol, from the Arabic word for 'demon'.

*The brown dwarf i...
by gravity to this ...
and brighter red ...*

> "Classifying the stars has
> helped materially in all studies of
> the structure of the Universe..."
>
> **Annie Jump Cannon (1863–1941)**
> *American astronomer*

Brown dwarf

Brown dwarfs are dim
objects, heavier than pla...
but lighter than true stars.
Strangely, although their
masses range from 20 to 80
times that of Jupiter, they
are all about the same size.

⊖ PULSATING STARS

Astronomers can work out the average true brightnesses of Cepheid stars, which are pulsating stars, from the times they take to fade and brighten. Taking into account the fact that all stars look dimmer the further away they are, the scientists can then work out the stars' distances from Earth.

A pulsating star is hottest and brightest when it is small.

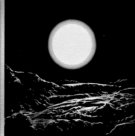

As the star swells, it fades, cools and reddens.

Some stars take only a few hours to swell and shrink; others take several years.

DEATH

Stars are like factories, converting hydrogen to helium, and helium to other elements, and producing floods of energy to light our skies by day and night. This nuclear-processing may continue steadily for billions of years. However, eventually, further conversion of elements becomes impossible, and stars die. But they don't go quietly...

When there is no fuel left to burn, the outer layers of a red giant swell, forming a bubble-like 'planetary nebula' (which has nothing to do with planets).

The nebula is made of such thin gas that its core – a white dwarf – can be seen. The white dwarf, which will take billions of years to cool, is the final stage in the life of medium and small-sized stars.

When the hydrogen fuel in the core of stars with a similar mass to the Sun runs out, nuclear reactions in outer layers take over. This causes the star to swell and cool, turning it into a red giant.

The Hourglass Nebula was probably shaped by wind expansion in a cloud that was more dense at its poles than at its equator.

Stars burn for millions or billions of years – the more massive they are, the more quickly they burn up and the shorter their lives.

Two paths to death

What happens when a star dies depends on its mass. Stars like the Sun swell enormously, melting and engulfing their closest planets (see path from left to above). More massive stars die in supernova explosions brighter than galaxies (see path from left to right). Supernovae can both trigger the birth of new stars and provide the building materials for them.

When they run out of hydrogen, massive stars swell up into supergiants – perhaps a million times the volume of the Sun and a hundred thousand times brighter. Many supergiants are pulsating variables, brightening as they shrink and fading as they swell.

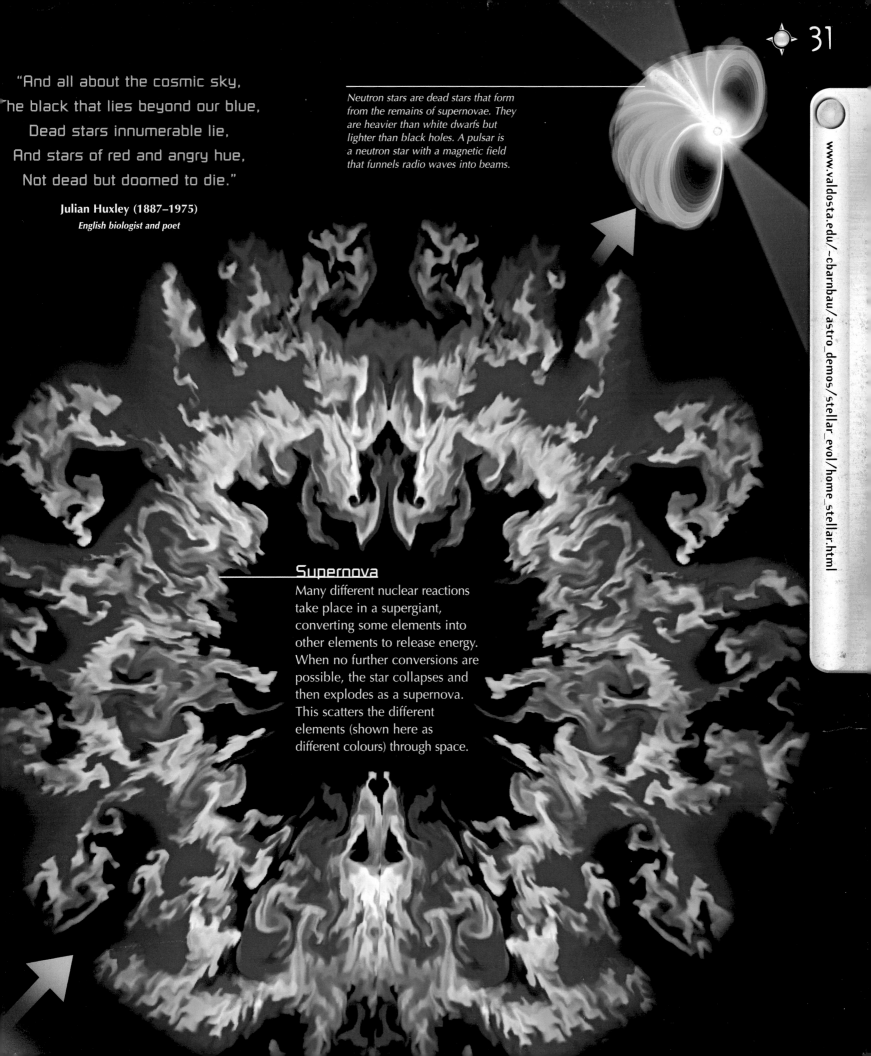

"And all about the cosmic sky,
he black that lies beyond our blue,
Dead stars innumerable lie,
And stars of red and angry hue,
Not dead but doomed to die."

Julian Huxley (1887–1975)
English biologist and poet

Neutron stars are dead stars that form
from the remains of supernovae. They
are heavier than white dwarfs but
lighter than black holes. A pulsar is
a neutron star with a magnetic field
that funnels radio waves into beams.

www.valdosta.edu/~cbarnbau/astro_demos/stellar_evol/home_stellar.html

Supernova

Many different nuclear reactions
take place in a supergiant,
converting some elements into
other elements to release energy.
When no further conversions are
possible, the star collapses and
then explodes as a supernova.
This scatters the different
elements (shown here as
different colours) through space.

Not all black holes
are deadly. If a black hole
spins fast enough, a spacecraft
on the correct route could take
a shortcut to another part of the
Universe – or even to another time.

SPACE WARPS

WARP – *a distortion or twist*

A century ago, Einstein showed that space and time are locked together into spacetime, and that spacetime is warped around massive objects. These warps are what we usually call gravity. The smooth warps made by the Sun guide the planets in their orbits – but not all space warps are so gentle…

Spacetime

Imagine spacetime as a stretched rubber sheet. Stars and planets warp the sheet as they sink into it. A fast object passing through a dip in spacetime will change direction, while a slower one will roll around the inside of the dip in orbit. An even slower object will spiral down into the dip.

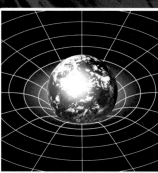

Wormholes

The more mass there is, the more warped spacetime becomes. If enough mass is concentrated into a small area, it can push through the folds of spacetime like a needle. This creates a connection between one place and time in the Universe and another – a wormhole.

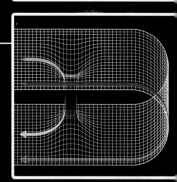

> The Universe is full of wormholes too tiny to see.

http://hubblesite.org/explore_astronomy/black_holes

The gravity near a black hole changes greatly over short distances, distorting nearby objects into long thin shapes before dragging them in. This is called spaghettification.

Black hole

In a normal star, the pull of gravity inwards is balanced by the pressure of radiation outwards. But when the star's fuel is exhausted and the radiation fades, gravity can no longer be resisted and the star collapses inwards. This causes the star's density to grow, and as it grows, the pull of its gravity increases. Eventually, in the most massive stars, all nearby objects are dragged into the star. Even light cannot escape the pull, so the star becomes black – a black hole.

SPACE PIONEERS

After the USSR surprised the world by reaching space first, the USA competed with them to send machines, animals and finally humans into orbit and onto the Moon. Space travel has many practical benefits, but it is also the urge to explore the unknown Universe that drives people onwards – and outwards, to other worlds.

escape rocket
(for use in a
launch emergency)

Apollo 11's command
module (under a
protective covering)

service module

Sputnik

On 4 October 1957, satellite *Sputnik 1*, an 84kg sphere, was blasted into space from the USSR. The first artificial object to orbit Earth, the beep of its radio transmitter could be picked up all over the planet. The Space Age had begun.

The lunar
module, Eagle,
is inside this
section.

aerial for transmitting
radio signals to Earth

Every nine seconds, the *Saturn V* rocket burnt enough fuel to fill a swimming pool.

Apollo 11: mission to the Moon

The lunar landing in 1969 was perhaps the most important event in history – the Moon is the first new world we have reached. The enormous *Saturn V* rocket launched the *Apollo 11* spaceship and its three-man crew across more than 300,000km of space. One after another, the three sections of the *Saturn V* ran out of fuel and were left behind, leaving the three Apollo modules to continue their voyage to the Moon.

> The fastest that humans have ever travelled is 10.8km/s – the speed that the crew of *Apollo 8* achieved in 1968.

USSR *the Union of Soviet Socialist Republics, or the Soviet Union (1922–1991). Russia was its largest member*

⊖ ESCAPE FROM EARTH

"That's one small step for a man; one giant leap for mankind."

Neil Armstrong (born 1930)
Commander of Apollo 11, 20 July 1969

Yuri Gagarin, a 27-year-old Russian pilot, became the first human in space in 1961. His *Vostok 1* spaceship, called *Swallow*, took him around Earth and returned him most of the way home: he parachuted the last few kilometres, landing in a farmer's field.

Gagarin waits to be launched into space.

http://news.bbc.co.uk/onthisday/hi/themes/science_and_technology/space

command module

service module

Journey's end

After a three-day journey, *Apollo 11*'s command-and-service module (CSM) reached the Moon and went into orbit around it. Astronauts Armstrong and Aldrin moved into the lunar module, *Eagle*, and piloted it down to the surface, leaving Collins onboard the CSM.

Apollo 17's CSM (above) was similar to Apollo 11's.

The Eagle has landed

The astronauts guided the lunar module, *Eagle*, to a safe landing on the Moon's Sea of Tranquillity.

thruster (one of four)

fuel tank

Only this top section of the Eagle returned to the CSM. The rest is still on the Moon.

foil to reflect sunlight and stop the Eagle overheating

landing pad

Aldrin, standing on the Moon, checks equipment on the Eagle.

BEYOND THE SKY

The rockets that took men to the Moon were enormous – and enormously expensive. And they could be used only once. For regular trips to the region of space near Earth, whether to repair satellites or visit space stations, craft that can be reused are needed.

Shuttles had large launch bays for transporting satellites and equipment, which were lifted into orbit by a robotic arm.

The external tank contained liquid fuel. After use, it was released and burned up in the atmosphere.

 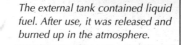 In space, the shuttle's robotic arm could move satellites more massive than lorries, but on Earth, it could not even lift itself up.

The space shuttle

The space shuttle, created by US space agency NASA, was a reusable spaceship that could orbit Earth. It was used for launching, retrieving and repairing satellites, travelling to space stations and for research. It took off like a rocket, but landed back on Earth like an aeroplane. During the 30 year shuttle programme, there were 135 missions. The last shuttle to touch down was *Atlantis*, in July 2011.

www.nasa.gov/mission_pages/shuttle/vehicle/index.html

Shuttle astronauts used nitrogen thrusters to move freely in space.

When their solid fuel had burned up, the two rocket boosters fell to Earth by parachute. They were refilled and reused.

328KF

SpaceShipOne

SCALED COMPOSITES

New horizons

The Orion spaceship is being developed to travel not only to the International Space Station (ISS) but to the Moon and Mars as well. Like the shuttle, it is a reusable craft.

SpaceShipOne

SpaceShipOne is an experimental space-plane launched in 2004. It reached a height of over 100km and flew more than three times faster than the speed of sound. A larger, more powerful version named *SpaceShipTwo* is now the basis of a commercial spaceflight programme.

The tail folds upwards on re-entry into Earth's atmosphere to reduce speed.

CITIES IN THE SKY

People are living high above your head right now, in the International Space Station (ISS), the latest in a series of space stations, which began in 1971 with the Soviet *Salyut 1*. The Americans followed with *Skylab*, an orbiting laboratory, in 1973. Today, space stations are used mainly for space research, but in future they will be hotels – and the first stepping stone for long-distance space explorers.

"Earth is the cradle of humanity, but one cannot live in the cradle forever."

Konstantin Tsiolkovsky (1857–1935)
Russian rocket scientist

Spinning through space

The International Space Station orbits Earth, but in the future, stations could use the energy of the Sun to power themselves on long missions to other worlds. Generations of explorers could live their whole lives onboard, harnessing the Sun's light and warmth to grow food. A spinning craft like this one would generate its own gravity for its inhabitants.

Onboard the ISS

The ISS is being constructed in orbit by 16 countries. Onboard, the astronauts and other objects are almost weightless, and the effects of this 'microgravity' on people, plants, crystals, fluids and flames will be studied, helping to plan future space colonies. Day-to-day life in the ISS is a constant experiment in weightlessness. Without the resistance of gravity, astronauts must exercise to stop their bones and muscles weakening. In 2007, astronaut Sunita Williams ran a marathon on the ISS's treadmill.

> The longest spaceflight – by Russian cosmonaut Valeriy Polyakov on the space station *Mir* – was 437 days long.

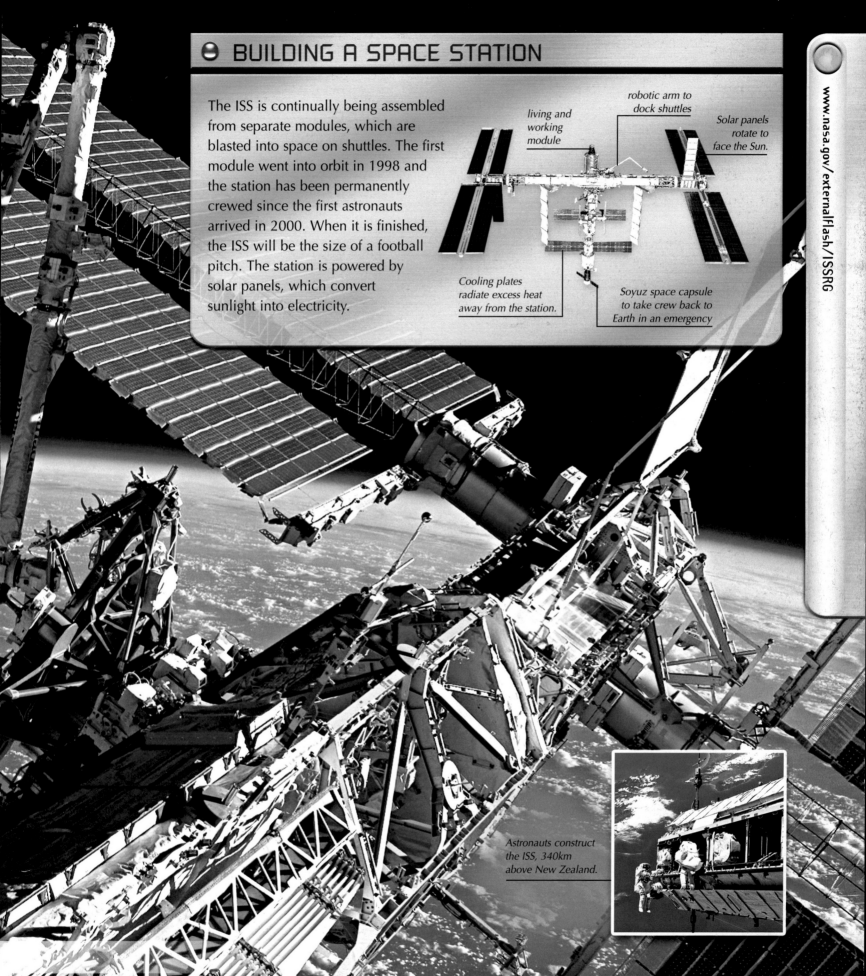

⊖ BUILDING A SPACE STATION

The ISS is continually being assembled from separate modules, which are blasted into space on shuttles. The first module went into orbit in 1998 and the station has been permanently crewed since the first astronauts arrived in 2000. When it is finished, the ISS will be the size of a football pitch. The station is powered by solar panels, which convert sunlight into electricity.

living and working module

robotic arm to dock shuttles

Solar panels rotate to face the Sun.

Cooling plates radiate excess heat away from the station.

Soyuz space capsule to take crew back to Earth in an emergency

Astronauts construct the ISS, 340km above New Zealand.

www.nasa.gov/externalflash/ISSRG

STARSHIPS

Travelling to the stars is easy – in fact, the Pioneer and Voyager unmanned planetary probes are on their way now, heading for the furthest reaches of the Solar System and interstellar space beyond. So, crossing vast distances is not the problem. The challenge is not space, but time – the probes will travel for tens of thousands of years before reaching a star. So, for people to explore other star systems, faster ships are needed.

Mining in space

The raw materials to make and fuel starships could one day be mined from asteroids, some of which are made entirely of metal. Their low gravity would make the materials almost weightless, so they would be easy to remove. Here, four robot craft are moving an asteroid past Mars on its way to Earth.

Landing craft

Starships will not be designed to land on other worlds. Instead, crews will descend to planets in short-range shuttle craft that have streamlined shapes for flying through planetary atmospheres.

> The nearest star is about one million times further from Earth than the nearest planet.

The metal web generates an electromagnetic field to 'scoop up' interstellar gas (mostly hydrogen). The invisible field extends for many kilometres beyond the web.

Voyages may last for centuries, so astronauts are deep-cooled inside hibernation pods, allowing them to sleep for decades without ageing.

The antenna enables communication with Earth. As the ramjet accelerates, it provides artificial gravity for the crew. So, structures like this have to be strong and light to support their own weight.

crew area

hydrogen duct

shield to protect crew areas from radiation from reactors

Inside the nuclear reactors, two types of hydrogen (deuterium and tritium) undergo nuclear fusion. This produces neutrons, helium and energy to power the ramjet.

fuel tanks

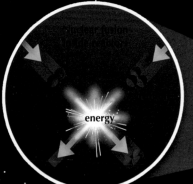

nuclear fusion

energy

Interstellar ramjet

All spaceships need not only fuel but material called reaction mass to blast away from them, so that they can thrust forwards in the opposite direction. To avoid carrying too much weight, an interstellar ramjet would draw in gas from space, use some of it as fuel for its nuclear reactors and some as reaction mass.

exhaust gases, including helium

LIFE BEYOND

Is Earth the only place where life exists? In search of an answer, robots sift the sands of Mars, signals are beamed to distant stars, probes carry messages on discs and plaques, and powerful radio telescopes scan the skies.

Worm-like animals prey on the microscopic creatures that cluster around the volcanic vents. The vents provide the warmth that living things need.

Free-swimming organisms use light to communicate.

> Germ-like structures have been found in a Martian meteorite.

Life on a distant moon?

The moon Europa is warmed by the gravity of Jupiter, the planet it orbits. This means that under its icy surface a vast ocean lies hidden. In its warm darkness, it is just possible that life exists. On Earth, too, there are creatures in the deep ocean that obtain their energy from underground heat.

The robot probe has sensors, thrusters and grippers.

The transporter has drilled and melted its way from Europa's icy surface.

⊜ POSTCARDS TO ALIENS

SIGNALS TO THE STARS ⊜

The space probes *Pioneer 10* and *Pioneer 11*, which were launched in 1972 and 1973 respectively, each carry a steel plate with picture-messages for any creatures that might find them.

humans, in front of diagram of probe to show scale

star map showing Sun's position in galaxy

Solar System

image on a plaque onboard the *Pioneer 10* probe

Earth's population in 1974: 4.2 billion

human

average height of human: 1,764mm

Sun and planets of our solar system

Arecibo telescope

part of the binary-coded Arecibo message

In 1974, the Arecibo radio telescope sent this message to a large group of stars. It will arrive there in about 27,000CE. (Colour has been added here to show the different pictures.)

GLOSSARY

antenna
A radio antenna, or aerial, is a device that sends or receives radio signals.

asteroid
A small rocky or metallic world orbiting the Sun. Asteroids are mainly found between the orbits of Mars and Jupiter.

atmosphere
Layer of gases around a star, planet or moon.

atom
The smallest part of an element, composed of a nucleus made of protons and neutrons. Electrons are arranged around the nucleus.

axis
An imaginary line that passes through the poles of a planet and on which a planet spins.

cosmos
Another word for the Universe.

electromagnetic field
A combination of an electric field and a magnetic field. Light and other types of radiation are a type of moving electromagnetic field.

element
A substance made of atoms that all have the same number of protons.

energy
Energy is what is required for work to be done, such as lifting an object. There are many types of energy, including sound, light, heat, electricity and mass.

galaxy
A large number of stars, together with planets, gas, dust and dark matter, held together by gravity.

gravity
A force that attracts all objects towards one another. The strength of the force depends on the objects' masses.

greenhouse effect
A process by which certain gases in the atmosphere of a planet trap some of the Sun's heat. As a result, the temperature of the planet rises.

helium
A very light substance, which is a gas at all but the lowest temperatures.

hemisphere
Half of a sphere.

hydrogen
A very light substance, the most common in the Universe. Most stars are made mainly of hydrogen.

Kuiper Belt object
A lump of ice and other frozen material in orbit beyond Neptune.

lunar
Relating to the Moon.

magnetic field
An area surrounding a moving electric charge or a magnet that produces pushes and pulls on other magnets, charges and other objects.

mass
A measure of the amount of matter in an object. In a gravitational field, the more mass an object has, the heavier it is.

matter
Substance that has mass and takes up space. Matter exists in four main forms: solid, liquid, gas and plasma. Particles of antimatter have opposite properties to those of matter. Dark matter is a mysterious substance known to exist only because of the effects of its gravity on ordinary matter.

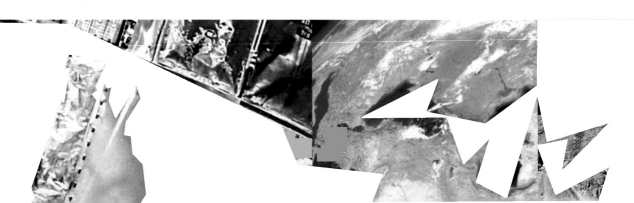

meteor

A meteor is the trail of light in the sky caused by a piece of rock or metal falling from space and burning up in our atmosphere. A meteoroid is the name given to the object before it falls. If part of the object reaches Earth's surface, it is called a meteorite.

moon

A moon is a world that orbits a planet.

nebula

A space object that looks like a cloud. Planetary nebulae are clouds of gas, often round, thrown off by dying stars. They are not connected with planets.

neutrino

A particle, much smaller than an atom, that exists in enormous numbers. They can pass through almost everything – even Earth – without stopping. Neutrinos are almost impossible to detect.

neutron

A neutron is a particle found in the nucleus of every atom except for hydrogen. A neutron star is a dead star in which the gravity is so high that its protons and electrons are crushed together and turn into neutrons.

nuclear

Nuclear means 'relating to the nucleus of an atom'. Nuclear fusion is the process in which hydrogen is converted to helium in the Sun and most stars, releasing the energy we see as sunlight and starlight.

nucleus

The core of an atom.

orbit

The path of one object around another in space, such as a planet around a star.

particle

A tiny fragment of matter.

probe

An uncrewed spaceship sent to explore other worlds and gather information.

proton

A particle with a positive electric charge found in the nuclei of all atoms.

radar

A system in which radio waves are beamed towards objects. The way they bounce back tells us about the object. Radar is used to track moving objects, map the surfaces of planets and to measure their distances from Earth.

radiation

A form of energy that travels through space as electromagnetic waves. Light, radio, infrared, ultraviolet, X-rays and gamma rays are all types of radiation.

radio

A form of electromagnetic radiation, with waves much longer than light waves.

satellite

An object in orbit around a planet. A moon is a natural satellite; a weather satellite is an artificial one.

solar panel

Solar means 'relating to the Sun'. A solar panel is a device that converts sunlight into heat or electricity.

star

A glowing mass of gas, held together by gravity.

supernova

A type of exploding star.

volume

A measure of the amount of space that something occupies.

INDEX

A

Aldrin, 'Buzz' 35
alien life 18, 42–43
Andromeda Galaxy 8
antennae 5, 19, 23, 41, 44
antimatter 6, 44
Apollo missions 34–35
Arecibo message 43
Armstrong, Neil 35
asteroids 24, 25, 40, 44
astronauts 35, 36, 37, 38, 39, 41
atmosphere (of Earth) 4, 12, 16, 24, 36
atmospheres 13, 14, 15, 20, 22, 24, 29, 40, 44
atoms 7, 26, 30, 44, 45
aurorae 12
axes 4, 17, 44

B

Barringer Crater 25
Big Bang 6, 7
Big Chill theory 7
Big Rip theory 7
binary stars 29
black holes 31, 32–33
blue giant stars 28
brown dwarf stars 29

C

Callisto 20
carbon stars 28
Charon 24
comets 11, 24, 25
cosmos 6, 44
craters 14, 19, 24, 25

D

dark energy 6
dark matter 6, 44
days (lengths of) 10, 11, 17, 20
dwarf planets 24

E

Eagle 35
Eagle Nebula 26
Earth 4, 5, 10, 12, 13, 14, 15, 16–17, 19, 24, 25, 27, 28, 29, 36, 37, 38, 40, 43, 44, 45
Einstein 32
electromagnetic fields 44
electrons 6, 7, 44, 45
elements 6, 7, 30, 31, 44
energy 6, 12, 23, 30, 31, 41, 44
Europa 20, 43

European Space Agency (ESA) 18, 19
ExoMars rover 18

G

Gagarin, Yuri 35
galaxies 6, 7, 8–9, 26, 44
Ganymede 20
gas giants 20, 22
gravity 6, 10, 20, 21, 22, 23, 32, 33, 38, 40, 41, 43, 44, 45
greenhouse effect 15, 44

H

Hale-Bopp 24
helium 6, 7, 12, 30, 41, 44, 45
hemispheres 17, 44
Herschel, William 22, 23, 27
Hourglass Nebula 30
Hubble Space Telescope 4–5
hydrogen 6, 7, 12, 30, 41, 44, 45

I

ice 10, 16, 19, 20, 23, 24

ice caps 18
International Space Station (ISS) 37, 38–39
Io 20

J

Jupiter 10, 20–21, 43, 44

K

Kitt Peak National Observatory 4
Kuiper Belt 11, 24, 44

M

Maat Mons 15
Magellan probe 15
magnetic fields 12, 13, 21, 31, 44
Mariner 10 10, 14
Mars 10, 16, 18–19, 37, 40, 42, 44
Mars Express Orbiter 19
matter 6, 44, 45
Mercury 10, 14
meteorites 24, 42, 45
meteoroids 24, 45
meteors 24, 45
Milky Way 9
Mimas 24

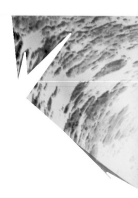

shining 40
Miranda 22
Moon (of Earth) 13, 34, 35, 44
moons 10, 20, 22, 23, 24, 43, 45

N

NASA 37
nebulae 26–27, 45
Neptune 11, 22, 23, 24, 44
neutrinos 5, 6, 45
neutron stars 31, 45
neutrons 41, 44, 45
nuclear reactions 12, 26, 30, 31, 41, 45
nuclei 30, 44, 45

O

observatories 4, 5
Oort Cloud 11
orbiting 9, 15, 22, 29, 43, 45
orbiting (Earth) 5, 34, 37, 39
orbiting (Sun) 12, 17, 22, 24, 32
Orion Nebula 27
Orion spaceship 37
oxygen 16, 18

P

Pillars of Creation 26–27
Pioneer probes 10, 11, 40, 43
planetary nebulae 27, 30, 45
planets 7, 9, 10–11, 14–23, 24, 32, 43
Pluto 24
poles 12, 19, 30, 44
probes 10–11, 14, 15, 18, 19, 23, 40, 42, 43, 45
protons 7, 44, 45
pulsars 30, 31
pulsating stars 29, 30

R

radar 15, 19, 45
radiation 9, 21, 26, 28, 33, 44, 45
radio waves 4, 31, 45
ramjets 41
Reconnaissance Orbiter 19
red giant stars 30
rings 20, 21, 22, 23
rockets 34, 36, 37

S

satellites (artificial) 5, 34, 36, 37, 38, 45

Saturn 10, 11, 20, 21, 24
Saturn V 34
seasons 17, 18
shooting stars 24
solar eclipses 13
solar panels 4, 18, 19, 39, 45
solar prominences 13
solar sails 13, 25
Solar System 9, 10–11, 23, 24, 43
space shuttles 4, 36–37
space stations 36, 37, 38–39
SpaceShipOne 37
spaceships 36–37, 40–41, 45
spacetime 32
spaghettification 33
Sputnik 1 34
star death 26, 30–31
starbirth 8, 9, 26, 30
stars 4, 6, 7, 8, 9, 26–31, 32, 33, 40, 44, 45
Sun 6, 7, 10, 12–13, 14, 16, 22, 24, 28, 44, 45
sunspots 13
supergiant stars 27, 30, 31
Super-Kamiokande observatory 5
supernovae 7, 26, 27, 30–31, 45

T

telescopes 4, 15, 42, 43
time 6, 32
Triton 23

U

Universe 6–7, 8, 32, 44
Uranus 11, 22, 23

V

variable stars 29, 30
Venus 10, 14, 15, 16
Viking 2 18
volcanoes 15, 17, 18
volume 10, 11, 45
Vostok 1 35
Voyager probes 11, 23, 40

W

Whirlpool Galaxy 8–9
white dwarf stars 30, 31
wormholes 32

Y

years (lengths of) 10–11, 14, 22

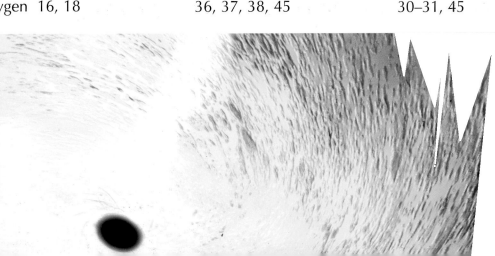

INVESTIGATE

Visit museums to learn about the history of space travel, and read books and websites to find out more about stars, the Universe and the planets in our solar system.

time-lapse image of a starry sky

Becoming an astronomer

Anyone can become an astronomer. You don't always need a telescope – stars, planets, satellites and galaxies can all be seen with the naked eye.

 Kingfisher Pocket Guides: Astronomy by Carole Stott (Kingfisher)

 Greenwich Royal Observatory, National Maritime Museum, London SE10 9NF

 www.schoolsobservatory.org.uk

tellation of Orion, the hunter

Constellations

Find out about the myths and legends behind each constellation – a group of stars representing an object, person, animal or even a monster.

 Stars and Constellations by Dr Raman K Prinja (Heinemann)

 Planetarium, Explore-At-Bristol, Anchor Road, Harbourside, Bristol BS1 5DB

http://library.thinkquest.org/3645/constellations.html

London's Science Museum

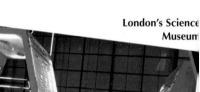

Space exploration

Take a trip to a space or science museum to discover how humans and uncrewed probes have travelled through space.

 Kingfisher Voyages: Space by Dr Mike Goldsmith (Kingfisher)

 The Science Museum, Exhibition Road, London SW7 2DD

www.bbc.co.uk/science/space/exploration

vision programmes and films bring space to life.

Television and media

Travel into space by watching real film footage recorded by astronauts or probes. And watch science-fiction films to spark your imagination about other worlds and alien life!

 Cinematic History of Sci-Fi and Fantasy by Mark Wilshin (Raintree)

 Stay at home and watch a DVD: *The Planets* (BBC)

www.bbc.co.uk/science/space